TO:

_____

FROM:

_____

DATE:

_____

INVULNERABLE MOMENTS

Meditations for Awakening Your Spiritual Power and Health

Dr. Priscilla Gathoni

Copyright © Dr. Priscilla Gathoni 2023

© All rights reserved. No part of this book may be reproduced in any form without permission in writing from the copyright owner, except in the case of brief quotations in critical articles or reviews.

ISBN 979-8-9895794-2-6 Paperback

ISBN 979-8-9895794-1-9 Hardcover

ISBN 979-8-9895794-0-2 eBook

Library of Congress Control Number: 2023908650

Table of Contents

Dedication 2

Preface 3

Introduction 5

Meditations for Power 9

Meditations for Riches 14

Meditations for Wisdom 19

Meditations for Strength 24

Meditations for Glory 29

Meditations for Honor 34

Meditations for Blessing 41

Affirmations 46

About the Author 49

Notes 50

Notes 51

Notes 52

Dedication

The author dedicates this book to all earnest and sincere of the human race engaged in a conscious effort to make themselves better and to make this world a better place to live in - a world freely expressed in health and happiness to complete a harmonious living.

Preface

In Him, we live and move, and have our being that I AM because He is; He is Omnipresent, and He is in me. That He is all in all, and I am in Him. That He is Spirit, and I am created in His image and likeness, and the difference between His Spirit and my Spirit is one of degree, that a part must be the same in kind and quality as the Whole.

Although Christian in statement, the meditations in Invulnerable Moments provide a universal experience and deal with universal spiritual themes that lead to God, the Universal Supreme Being, the Great Architect of the Universe. Therefore, allow your Internal Teacher to direct your meditation efforts and guide you to Wholeness. You will receive your Internal Teacher's gifts that make you perfectly invulnerable. The meditations allow the harmonious interaction of the conscious and subconscious levels of the mind. Allow the infinite intelligence of your subconscious mind to draw out the hidden inspiration and wisdom within you.

The law of belief operates in all religions of the world, and these meditations used as prayers will bring about the realization of your heart's desire. We get answers to our prayers, not because of a particular creed, religion, ritual, sacrifices, or offerings, but solely because of belief or mental acceptance and receptivity about that which we are praying for. Speak to Him, thou, for He listens, and Spirit with Spirit can meet; closer to Him than breathing you are, nearer than hands and feet.

The 108 meditations in this book are suitable for all ages, and their nature can bring healing, freedom, happiness, and peace of mind, and sever you from emotional and physical bondage. Read them aloud to your children to help them learn how to use their inner power as they grow up. Enjoy the meditations and let incredible wonders happen in your life!

To you, O Spirit of God, I turn and ask that Infinite Power, Wisdom, Riches, Strength, Glory, Honor, and Blessing may grow and increase within each person that reads this book. May these Eternal gifts flow into all their learning, work, thoughts, words, actions, habits, character, and destiny at all times, everywhere. I rejoice and give thanks, for I know it is so.

Introduction

Spirit is all there is. The mind that serves the Spirit is invulnerable. Life's purpose is to grow the gifts that Spirit has given us freely. Spirit's only activity is the power to think; since Spirit is creative, thoughts must be creative. This creative power of thought is impersonal, universal, and at our immediate disposal and control. Thinking is a spiritual activity. Our business in life should be to use this creative power of thought for our benefit and for the benefit of humanity.

The gifts given to us by the Holy Spirit (also referred to as the Great Eternal Spirit, Divine Spirit, Pure Spirit, and Spirit of God) are Power, Riches, Wisdom, Strength, Glory, Honor, and Blessing. Seeking the Divine Spirit to grow these fruits within you and for you is your ultimate goal here on earth, your Spiritual Health. The evidence of these gifts is necessary to show the Divine Presence that controls and gives without favor that each of us has been endowed with. What makes us different from the animal kingdom is our power of thought and the ability to clothing words into sentences, thus making the human being a part of the Omnipotence. Such gifts are rare to most people because they do not know how to use the Spiritual Power they have been given. Any power must be used, otherwise, it lacks essence. The essence flows by continuous use of this marvelous power, which, in turn, blossoms your spiritual health.

What, then, is essential for you as a human being? Is it harboring discordant thoughts that bring destruction and devastation to you? What should you think, and what are your predominant thoughts? How can you change these thoughts for your good? What does the law of cause and effect tell you? What is your relationship with the Universal Mind? Have you found peace and harmony in your life? The law of Love supersedes all laws, and these questions can be answered and solutions made clear to all those who have the burning desire, the courage to dare, and the faith to do.

This book will explore these wonderful gifts meditatively and offer you short prayers to grow these gifts in your life now in order to be ready to harvest the first fruits of their kind. These prayers will awaken your power of thought and unlock the storehouse of wisdom when practiced daily. When you resolve to be a daily practitioner, you will rise up above all the challenges that come your way. Your spiritual race is blessed, and the fruits of faith, love, hope, peace, bliss, abundance, and contentment are ready for you, both now and forever. Life will change to a new and fulfilling adventure that only a select few will be able to say, in all honesty, that life is more than wonderful and they live in a most wonderful world.

The Holy and Divine Essence within you will guide, direct, heal, comfort, and prosper you spiritually, mentally, and materially as you read and meditate. Love is the eternal gift you can have and give!

Dr. Priscilla Gathoni

Meditations For Power

Meditations for Power

1

Holy Spirit, open for me heart and sensing soul so that I may be strong to understand that great goodness and proclaim the wonderful works and virtue that form the doorway to all inspiration, both now and forevermore. I give thanks, for I know it is so.

2

Great Eternal Spirit, abide in me and allow this day to be filled with your goodness and virtue. Restore and nurture our minds for those things that build, grow, and revitalize our soul and body, both now and forevermore. I give thanks for I know it is so.

3

Spirit of God, guide my actions this day to be pure and selfless, empty my mind and heart of all unworthy thoughts, words, and deeds so that I may preserve a conscience void of offense towards God and all the people I meet today, both now and forevermore. I give thanks, for I know it is so.

4

Holy Spirit, abide within us this day and grant us the wisdom to know that which is good and great for the glory of The Most High, both now and forevermore. I give thanks, for I know it is so.

5

Spirit of God, I step confidently into the blank of my mind and allow you to strengthen my resolutions, guide me to hold onto the Center, and finally find the Truth within, both now and forevermore. I give thanks, for I know it is so.

6

Great Eternal Spirit, allow your infinite wisdom and strength to nourish our souls this day and reveal to us the inexhaustible power that resides within us, both now and forevermore. I give thanks, for I know it is so.

7

Spirit of God, allow your infinite power to guide me and reveal to me everything I need to know at all times, everywhere. I give thanks, for I know it is so.

8

Holy Spirit, filll my inner garment this day with infinite love, power, strength, wisdom, and courage to follow the inner callings within me that are infinite, universal, immortal, beautiful, and endures forever, both now and forevermore. I give thanks, for I know it is so.

9

Spirit of God, my entire being is open to listen to your voice in all my undertakings, reveal your presence and bring me to my infinite perfection, which endures forever. I give thanks, for I know it is so.

10

Holy Spirit, thank you for guiding me and directing my soul to be humble and selfless in all my affairs, both now and forevermore. I give thanks, for I know it is so.

11

Great Eternal Spirit, guide me to move in harmony with the present moment to be gentle and kind in dealing with others, to stand by my word, to govern with equity, and to be timely in choosing the right moment, both now and forevermore. I give thanks, for I know it is so.

12

Spirit of God, increase in me that divine wisdom that recognizes each day is a new life, and to stop pouring when my cup is full, and to rest when my cup is empty, both now and forevermore. I give thanks, for I know it is so.

13

Great Eternal Spirit, renew my strength, wisdom, and knowledge, and fill my cup with infinite goodness and virtue that comes only from you, both now and forevermore. I give thanks, for I know it is so.

14

Spirit of God, guide me to be selfless in all my undertakings and to uphold the virtues of fortitude and fidelity in everything I do, both now and forevermore. I give thanks, for I know it is so.

15

Great Eternal Spirit, nourish my soul this day, restore the integrity of my mind to be at one with God, and allow my thoughts to be carried by the great wave of your infinite creative power, both now and forevermore. I give thanks for I know it is so.

Meditations For Riches

Meditations for Riches

1

Holy Spirit, guide me to appreciate the usefulness of the sacred space within me and the emptiness without, both now and forevermore. I give thanks, for I know it is so.

2

Almighty and Eternal Father, make me a vessel of honor, integrity, power, love, faith, hope, beauty, strength, and wisdom to perform the wonderful works that God has called me to be and to do, both now and forevermore. I give thanks for I know it is so.

3

Great Eternal Spirit, nourish my soul this day and guide me to be a master observer of the world, and to trust my inner vision, and allow things and people to come and go, keeping only what is sacred within me, both now and forevermore. I give thanks, for I know it is so.

4

Holy Spirit, fashion worthily my soul this day to be a fitting raiment for your wonderful works, both now and forevermore. I give thanks, for I know it is so.

5

Great Eternal Spirit, guide my thoughts, words, and actions this day and grant me wisdom and strength to subdue the ego in all my undertakings, both now and forevermore. I give thanks, for I know it is so.

6

Spirit of God, allow this day to be filled with your inexhaustible and infinite power, riches, wisdom, strength, glory, honor, and blessing; may these wonderful gifts be felt and materialized within each soul in the world, both now and forevermore. I give thanks, for I know it is so.

7

Holy Spirit, guide my thoughts, words, and actions this day to be impartial, peaceful, insightful, creative, and to be in a state of gratitude at all times and everywhere. I give thanks, for I know it is so.

8

Almighty and Eternal God, Ruler and Architect of the universe, we supplicate the continual flowing of your power that allows us to be divine, to be born into eternal life, and at one with the Holy Spirit, both now and forevermore. I give thanks, for I know it is so.

9

Holy Spirit, allow your greatness to flourish within me, in me, for me, and through me. I come from greatness, I attract greatness, and I am greatness, both now and forevermore. I give thanks, for I know it is so.

10

Great Eternal Spirit, help me realize my true nature today and fulfill the dream of my Divine Creator, to live to my highest calling, and be pressed by the mark of my highest calling, both now and forevermore. I give thanks, for I know it is so.

11

Spirit of God, guide me this day to temper desire, cast off selfishness, allow simplicity and kindness of heart to guide my actions, and to realize my true spiritual nature, both now and forevermore. I give thanks, for I know it is so.

12

Holy Spirit, thank you for guiding, directing, comforting, healing, and abiding in me, both now and forevermore. I give thanks, for I know it is so.

13

Spirit of God, thank you for being the Essence of my life, for rising up like a fountain, inexhaustible and ever-increasing in flow within me, at all times, everywhere. I give thanks, for I know it is so.

14

Great Eternal Spirit, thank you for the feeling of contentment with my life, thoughts of joy, and the gifts of love, sacrifice, wealth, and generosity, both now and forevermore. I give thanks, for I know it is so.

Meditations for Wisdom

Meditations for Wisdom

1

Great Eternal Spirit, increase in me wisdom, knowledge, sagacity, and inspiration to know myself as a leader, and to be a virtuous example to all I lead, both now and forevermore. I give thanks, for I know it is so.

2

Holy Spirit, thank you for restoring the Essence of life within me, healing, guiding, and comforting me, both now and forevermore. I give thanks, for I know it is so.

3

Spirit of God, enrich our souls this day with your goodness and virtue, and fill our cups with infinite joy, peace, bliss, love, and gladness at all times and everywhere, both now and forevermore. I give thanks, for I know it is so.

4

Great Eternal Spirit, open my heart and sensing soul to receive the fountain of goodness and virtue at all times and everywhere, both now and forevermore. I give thanks, for I know it is so.

5

Holy Spirit, guide me this day to walk in the path that firmly binds my thoughts, words, and actions to ascend unpolluted to the Throne of God, both now and forevermore. I give thanks, for I know it is so.

6

Great Eternal Spirit, guide me this day to walk the path of enlightenment with firmness and confidence established and rooted only in you, both now and forevermore. I give thanks, for I know it is so.

7

Holy Spirit, thank you for allowing your wisdom to be boundless, eternally flowing, and constantly returning in me, through me, within me, and for me, both now and forevermore. I give thanks, for I know it is so.

8

Spirit of God, unlock the storehouse of wisdom for me this day to understand the greatness within me, both now and forevermore. I give thanks, for I know it is so.

9

Holy Spirit, thank you for unlocking the greatness within me and blessing me with Divine power, wisdom, knowledge, and inspiration, both now and forevermore. I give thanks, for I know it is so.

10

Great Eternal Spirit, increase in me that wisdom which knowest my truest interest, strengthen my resolution and understanding, to perform that which brings me closer to the path of Divine Light, both now and forevermore. I give thanks, for I know it is so.

11

Spirit of God, increase in me that Divine power and wisdom that discovers my truest interest and strengthen my resolution to perform that which the Spirit dictates, both now and forevermore. I give thanks, for I know it is so.

12

Great Eternal Spirit, guide me this day to fashion worthily my soul as a fitting raiment for your Divine work, both now and forevermore. I give thanks, for I know it is so.

13

Great Eternal Spirit, guide me to be the pattern of the world, to constantly move in the path of virtue, without erring a single step, to be the fountain of the world, and to constantly return again to the will of the Divine Creator with resignation and humility, both now and forevermore. I give thanks, for I know it is so.

14

Spirit of God, restore the qualities of virtue, goodness, kindness, equity, justice, and uprightness within me and everyone I come in contact with, today and forevermore. I give thanks, for I know it is so.

Meditations for Strength

Meditations for Strength

1

Great Eternal Spirit, nourish my soul this day and restore the integrity of my mind to be at one with God, and preserve the original qualities of being holy, sinless, perfect, and free as God created me, both now and forevermore. I give thanks, for I know it is so.

2

Holy Spirit, allow my life to unfold naturally this day, increase in me strength, knowledge, and wisdom, and allow my mind to be a vessel of perfection, both now and forevermore. I give thanks, for I know it is so.

3

Spirit of God, thank you for outpouring your guidance and strength to the leaders of this nation so that they may be attuned to the way of Light, both now and forevermore. I give thanks, for I know it is so.

4

Spirit of God, guide our steps this day and allow our highest nature to flourish, bringing peace and stillness to our minds, both now and forevermore. I give thanks, for I know it is so.

5

Spirit of God, strengthen my intellectual faculties and help me to advance in my thoughts and ideas in life, learning, and work, both now and forevermore. I give thanks, for I know it is so.

6

Great Eternal Spirit, abide in me this day and guide my thoughts to know when to stop, know when reason sets limit, and allow my thoughts to flow back to become one with God, both now and forevermore. I give thanks, for I know it is so.

7

Holy Spirit, I invite you to abide with me, and I surrender my life, work, learning, thoughts, words, actions, habits, character, and destiny in your capable hands, and I give thanks for all the wonderful things that God has blessed me with, both now and forevermore. I give thanks, for I know it is so.

8

Spirit of God, grant me the wisdom to understand myself, strength to master myself, beauty to know myself, and complete contentment with who and where I am, both now and forevermore. I give thanks, for I know it is so.

9

Holy Spirit, open the way for greatness and goodness this day and enrich my soul with thy virtue that I may know you more now and forevermore. I give thanks, for I know it is so.

10

Great Eternal Spirit, restore love, happiness, peace, bliss, and joy everlasting to all humanity this day, both now and forevermore. I give thanks, for I know it is so.

11

Holy Spirit, help me this day to seek out obscurity by suppressing all thoughts of pride and selfishness that leads to a flight from my allotted tasks here on earth, both now and forevermore. I give thanks, for I know it is so.

12

Holy Spirit, enter in my silence now and help me find the anchor of the universe within myself, both now and forevermore. I give thanks, for I know it is so.

13

Spirit of God, guide me this day to center my life, work, and thoughts in you, both now and forevermore. I give thanks, for I know it is so.

14

Great Eternal Spirit, thank you for granting me a vision for the future, unlocking the storehouse of wisdom, virtue, and peace everlasting, and prospering me with a life full of infinite spiritual power, both now and forevermore. I give thanks, for I know it is so.

Meditations For Glory

Meditations for Glory

1

Holy Spirit, direct my path of life to be rooted in humility, bend in resignation, and to live in accordance with the will of God, both now and forevermore. I give thanks, for I know it is so.

2

Spirit of God, allow the gentle wind of your goodness, kindness, and virtue to guide me, both now and forevermore. I give thanks, for I know it is so.

3

Great Eternal Spirit, guide me this day to return to the Divine Creator, and yield my life for the Almighty Architect to find celebration through me, both now and forevermore. I give thanks, for I know it is so.

4

Holy Spirit, nourish my soul this day and bring everything my heart desires to humble fulfillment to the Glory of God, both now and forevermore. I give thanks, for I know it is so.

5

Spirit of God, nourish my soul this day and allow the Glory of God to be felt in everything I do, say, and think, both now and forevermore. I give thanks, for I know it is so.

6

Great Eternal Spirit, open the eyes of my heart this day that I may discover the path of illumination with true clarity, power, love, and wisdom, both now and forevermore. I give thanks, for I know it is so.

7

Spirit of God, direct this day to be steeped in balance, peace, and harmony for me and everyone with whom I come in contact, both now and forevermore. I give thanks, for I know it is so.

8

Holy Spirit, direct me this day to keep down all vain and unbecoming thoughts that might obtrude in any of my undertakings so that my words and actions may ascend unpolluted to the Throne of God, both now and forevermore. I give thanks, for I know it is so.

9

Great Eternal Spirit, thank you for the abundance in the gifts of contentment, glory, sacrifice, and inspiration in my life, both now and forevermore. I give thanks, for I know it is so.

10

Holy Spirit, guide me this day to embrace stillness and tranquility and allow the perfection of my soul to rule my life, both now and forevermore. I give thanks, for I know it is so.

11

Spirit of God, thank you for giving me renewed faith, hope, love, the bliss of eternity, and a spirit of unconquerable contentment, both now and forevermore. I give thanks, for I know it is so.

12

Spirit of God, thank you for the gifts of wisdom and inspiration to look inward for peace, joy, love, bliss, happiness, and contentment that leads to a life of completion, both now and forevermore. I give thanks, for I know it is so.

13

Great Eternal Spirit, direct my thoughts, words, and actions this day to yield and let things go their own way, and may self-mastery be my resolution, both now and forevermore. I give thanks, for I know it is so.

14

Holy Spirit, guide me this day to follow the path of kindness, goodness, harmony, and faithfulness, and may these virtues direct my life and everyone I encounter, both now and forevermore. I give thanks, for I know it is so.

15

Spirit of God, increase in me the gifts of humility, empathy, patience, persistence, perseverance, overcoming, and victory each moment of my life, both now and forevermore. I give thanks, for I know it is so.

Meditations for Honor

Meditations for Honor

1

Holy Spirit, preserve the original qualities of being free, perfect, holy, and sinless as God created me. May the circumstances of this day bring completion, and may the honor of God nourish, nurture, shelter, and protect me, both now and forevermore. I give thanks, for I know it is so.

2

Spirit of God, guide me to set a watch at the entrance of my thoughts, place a guard at the door of my lips, post a sentinel at the avenue of my actions, seek clarity in my vision, and grant me the strength to return again to the Eternal Light, both now and forevermore. I give thanks, for I know it is so.

3

Great Eternal Spirit, increase my intellect, guide my steps to walk on the paths of Heavenly Science, and even closer to the Throne of God, both now and forevermore. I give thanks, for I know it is so.

4

Great Eternal Spirit, direct my life to be firmly planted in you, embrace your teachings in all my undertakings, allow virtue to be realized in all my affairs, and see you as my guiding Light by looking inside myself, both now and forevermore. I give thanks, for I know it is so.

5

Holy Spirit, guide my thinking, willing, and feeling to be in harmony with my words, actions, and habits; and allow insight, inspiration, sagacity, and wisdom to flow and increase in me, both now and forevermore. I give thanks, for I know it is so.

6

Spirit of God, guide me this day to rise above the cares of others that don't build or grow me, rise above judging others or things, rise above any form of attachment or resistance, and not to be swayed by emotions or common fears. Allow my heart and soul to dwell in your safety and abide in you, both now and forevermore. I give thanks, for I know it is so.

7

Great Eternal Spirit, strengthen my power of thought, grant me the wisdom to master myself, and surround me with beauty, both now and forevermore. I give thanks, for I know it is so.

8

Spirit of God, guide my thoughts, words, and actions this day, strengthen my resolution to stop controlling anyone or myself, and help me be content, peaceful, and to walk in God's will, both now and forevermore. I give thanks, for I know it is so.

9

Great Eternal Spirit, guide my path of life to be a master of my own fate, and not to impose my will on anyone or anything, and allow my mind and heart to embrace simplicity and purity, allowing the Eternal Light to shine through me and for me, both now and forevermore. I give thanks, for I know it is so.

10

Spirit of God, I give up my own ideas and let you lead the way, guide, direct, and allow my thoughts and actions to be deeply rooted and firmly planted in you, and may long life and lasting vision be my eternal gifts, both now and forevermore. I give thanks, for I know it is so.

11

Holy Spirit, I invite you to abide with me this day and direct my approach to all things to be in harmony with you, both now and forevermore. I give thanks, for I know it is so.

12

Great Eternal Spirit, guide me this day to lower myself in stillness, solitude, and quietness of your Voice, and let my words and actions bring friendship and trust to all the people I meet both now and forevermore. I give thanks, for I know it is so.

13

Spirit of God, guide me this day to meditate on the Principle that you are my Source of wisdom, strength, and beauty. Help me to awaken and elevate everyone I meet with my words and deeds, and to see God as the Great Advancing Presence in All and Good in All, both now and forevermore. I give thanks, for I know it is so.

14

Great Eternal Spirit, increase in me that wisdom that sees simplicity in the complicated, confront difficulties when they are still easy, and achieve greatness in everything I am, do, and say, both now and forevermore. I give thanks, for I know it is so.

15

Spirit of God, guide me, lead me, and help me to be open to new thoughts, ideas, and ideals, and to give as much care at the end as at the beginning, both now and forevermore. I give thanks, for I know it is so.

16

Great Eternal Spirit, increase in me infinite wisdom and contentment, purity of heart, and simplicity in my thoughts, words, and actions that I may serve as a Shining Light for anyone I come in contact with, both now and forevermore. I give thanks, for I know it is so.

17

Holy Spirit, fill my cup of virtue to overflowing and render the fullness of life to accompany me in all my undertakings, both now and forevermore. I give thanks, for I know it is so.

18

Spirit of God, grant this day to be filled with contentment, peace everlasting, bliss, humility, love for humanity, and unshakeable obedience to the inner voice that guides and directs us to a place of joy and bliss, both now and forevermore. I give thanks, for I know it is so.

Meditations For Blessing

Meditations for Blessing

1

Spirit of God, increase in me that humility and empathy which brings comfort, love, light, harmony, and peace to everyone that I lead, both now and forevermore. I give thanks, for I know it is so.

2

Great Eternal Spirit, thank you for protecting me with your infinite love in all my thoughts, words, actions, habits, character, and destiny, both now and forevermore. I give thanks, for I know it is so.

3

Spirit of God, direct my path this day to embrace employing the powers of others, not competing, not contending, but to achieve ultimate harmony and unity with all aspects of creation by exercising humility, and virtue at all times, everywhere; both now and forevermore. I give thanks, for I know it is so.

4

Spirit of God, guide me this day to recognize, realize, and nurture the "I" in me and allow wholesome, healthful, and harmonious conditions to prevail in me and for me, both now and forevermore. I give thanks, for I know it is so.

5

Great Eternal Spirit, fill my interior garment with the precious gems of spiritual character, wisdom, inspiration, knowledge, and power, both now and forevermore. I give thanks, for I know it is so.

6

Spirit of God, increase in me the knowledge and understanding of the creative power of thought so that my words and deeds may ascend unpolluted to the throne of God, both now and forevermore. I give thanks, for I know it is so.

7

Holy Spirit, abide with me and help me recognize that I am whole as God created me, and to embrace the fact that I am created in the image and likeness of God, both now and forevermore. I give thanks, for I know it is so.

8

Great Eternal Spirit, direct me this day to realize that the spiritual "I" within me is infinite, whole, and exuberant in wisdom, both now and forevermore. I give thanks, for I know it is so.

9

Spirit of God, awaken in me infinite love, wisdom, inspiration, knowledge, sagacity, and insatiable willpower today and forevermore. I give thanks, for I know it is so.

10

Great Eternal Spirit, awaken my spiritual intelligence to perform spiritual deeds, celebrate what is within me, and surround myself with your love each moment today, and forevermore. I give thanks for I know it is so.

11

Holy Spirit, increase in me that spiritual power, intelligence, and wisdom that enables me to know and understand myself, to surround my thoughts with love, and to continuously prefer what is within instead of what is without, both now and forevermore. I give thanks, for I know it is so.

12

Holy Spirit, direct me this day to say little, ask less, avoid hurry, and conquer negative thoughts without striving. Direct my thoughts, words, and actions to be bold and in harmony with you, both now and forevermore. I give thanks, for I know it is so.

13

Great Eternal Spirit, anoint this day to be a day of contemplation and gratitude for the wonderful gifts God has blessed me with, both now and forevermore. I give thanks, for I know it is so.

14

Spirit of God, abide with me this day, and allow unshakeable fidelity and courage to guide me, and reveal to me ideal thoughts free of fear and anxiety in all my affairs, both now and forevermore. I give thanks, for I know it is so.

15

Holy Spirit, comfort and anoint me to trust in you, and work with me to be the Light that shines continuously to bring love and understanding to everyone that I meet today. I give thanks, for I know it is so.

16

Great Eternal Spirit, open the eyes of our hearts this day to be soft and supple, flexible, and appreciative of the wonderful works of our Father who dwelleth in us, both now and forevermore. I give thanks, for I know it is so.

17

Spirit of God, thank you for allowing me this day to share the surplus Spiritual Power you have blessed me with for the greater good of humanity and the world, both now and forevermore. I give thanks, for I know it is so.

18

Holy Spirit, imbue this day with the Light of your great goodness and allow us to seek you in all our daily affairs. Impart thy grace and serenity to thy servants and guide us to dwell in your Infinite and Divine Presence, both now and forevermore. I give thanks, for I know it is so.

Affirmations

I am a Spiritual Being, blessed with Spiritual gifts to perform Spiritual deeds.

* * *

Divine Spirit, increase in me Spiritual Power to perform Spiritual deeds at all times, everywhere.

* * *

I am a blessed child of God, and what I am is Infinite; I do not judge the evolution of others, what they are right now is for their highest good.

* * *

My mind is a center of divine operation.

* * *

This moment is invulnerable, and I am one with all creation and my Divine Creator.

* * *

Contentment and balance are my eternal gifts, and I am truly rich and blessed.

* * *

Nothing is left undone. I now sleep in peace and awake with joy.

* * *

I have no questions in my mind. I now sleep in peace.

* * *

I am a wonderful and blessed child of God, limitless in creative energy, powerful, harmonious, happy, wholly loving, and wholly loveable.

* * *

I am a wonderful and great spiritual being that illuminates with Light everywhere I go and everyone I meet, at all times, everywhere.

* * *

I am completely free from all forms of destructive thoughts, habits, memories, and fears. Harmony, sobriety, and peace of mind reign supreme.

* * *

By day and by night, I am being prospered in all my interests and ways.

* * *

I am whole, perfect, strong, powerful, loving, harmonious, and happy.

* * *

My aim in life is peace, health, inspiration, harmony, and abundance.

* * *

I am happy, radiant, successful, serene, and powerful.

* * *

I am healthy, happy, vigorous, full of life, and enthusiasm.

* * *

I have the ability to stay poised, balanced, and centered regardless of what goes before me.

* * *

I am born of the Divine Creator, and my thoughts, words, and actions flow back to become one with my Divine Creator.

About the Author

Dr. Priscilla Gathoni is a versatile professional who excels in various roles. She is an executive coach, speaker, author, educator, and voice artist. With her captivating talks, she has left a lasting impression on audiences at global conferences, corporate and community events. As a coach, Dr. Gathoni is known for her energetic and engaging approach. She uses effective coaching tools and techniques to help clients unlock their true potential and achieve their goals. In addition to her coaching expertise, Dr. Gathoni is a Professor in Data Science at the University of Maryland Global Campus. Her personal research interests extend to spiritual leadership, knowledge leadership, and spiritual intelligence.

To learn more about Dr. Gathoni, please visit:

www.wakanyienterprises.com

Notes

This book inspires the human race to awaken their spiritual and mental powers through daily meditations.

Add your personal meditations here:

Notes

This book inspires the human race to awaken their spiritual and mental powers through daily meditations.

Add your personal meditations here:

Notes

This book inspires the human race to awaken their spiritual and mental powers through daily meditations.

Add your personal meditations here:

www.ingramcontent.com/pod-product-compliance
Lightning Source LLC
Chambersburg PA
CBHW051621010526
44119CB00009B/227